New Dimensions Spears
IN THE
WORLD OF READING

Out Came the Sun

P R O G R A M   A U T H O R S

James F. Baumann	Roselmina Indrisano	P. David Pearson
Theodore Clymer	Dale D. Johnson	Taffy E. Raphael
Carl Grant	Connie Juel	Marian Davies Toth
Elfrieda H. Hiebert	Jeanne R. Paratore	Richard L. Venezky

Contributing Author: Rosann Englebretson

COVER ILLUSTRATOR

Spotlight

Quang Ho

✦ Quang Ho loves the southwest and has painted the hoedown scene on the cover of this book. The animals are happy to see the sun after a rain and are enjoying a lively and colorful southwestern picnic.

✦ Quang was born in Vietnam, and grew up without any picture books. He read comic books and drew comic book people. He tells first graders, "Do a lot of reading! It helps you imagine what to draw."

SILVER BURDETT GINN

NEEDHAM, MA   MORRISTOWN, NJ
ATLANTA, GA   DALLAS, TX   DEERFIELD, IL   MENLO PARK, CA

Theme

How's the Weather?

Theme Books for
How's the Weather?

Is it rainy or sunny outside today?

✳ What makes the wind blow in *Feel the Wind* by Arthur Dorros?

✳ Enjoy a rainy-day walk through the puddles in *Rain Talk* by Mary Serfozo.

✳ Read *Ice Storm* by Jean Groce to see how a stormy day can be cozy.

✳ Find out where the animals live in *Who Lives Here?* by Katherine Mead.

✳ How can a bumbershoot keep you dry? Read *Does Your Grandpa Say Galoshes?* by Katherine Mead.

✳ It's stormy and Josephine is outside in *Josephine's Night Out* by D. Marion. Will she get home safely?

The Itsy Bitsy Spider

The itsy bitsy spider
went up the waterspout.

Down came the rain
and washed the spider out.

Out came the sun
and dried up all the rain.

And the itsy bitsy spider
went up the spout again.

8

Spring is Here

Taro Gomi

Spring is here.

The snow melts.

13

The earth is fresh.

15

The grass sprouts.

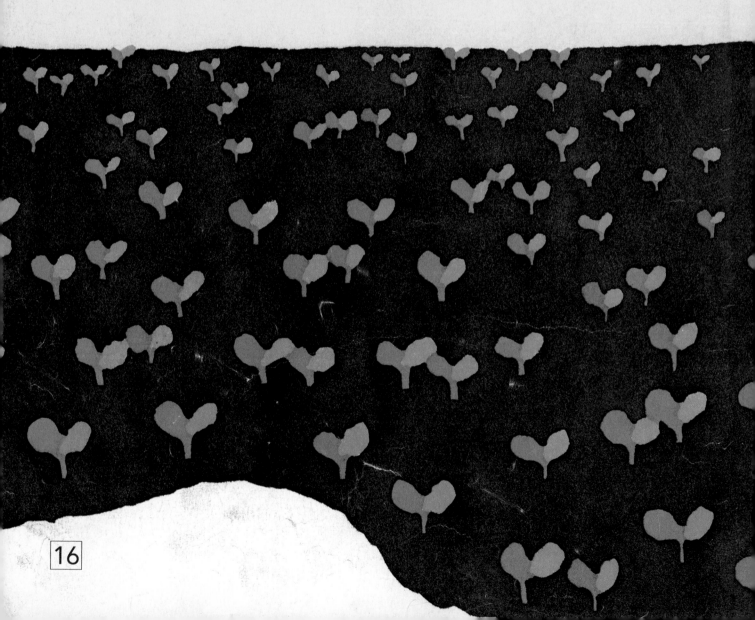

The flowers bloom.

18

The grass grows.

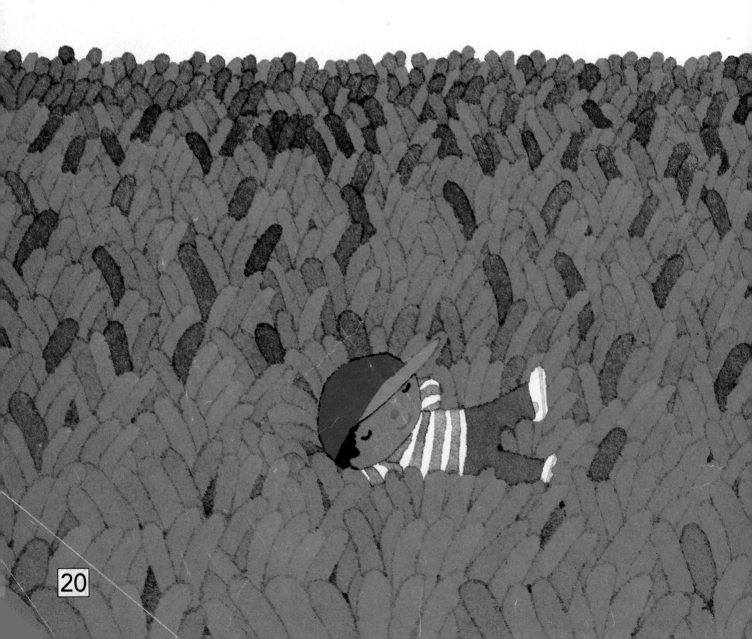

21

The winds blow.

The storms rage.

25

The quiet harvest arrives.

The snow falls.

The children play.

The world is hushed.

The world is white.

The snow melts.

The calf has grown.

39

Spring is here.

41

Just One More Puddle

written by Ethan Miles
illustrated by Scott Nash

"Christopher Anthony Jonathan Tuttle,
Don't you step in a single puddle!"

So Christopher Anthony Jonathan
changed his wet shoes
and went out again.

"Christopher Anthony Jonathan Tuttle,
Don't you step in ONE MORE puddle!"

44

So Christopher Anthony Jonathan
changed his wet shoes
and changed his wet socks
and went out again.

"Christopher Anthony Jonathan Tuttle,
Don't you step in ONE MORE puddle!"

So Christopher Anthony Jonathan
changed his wet pants
and changed his wet socks
and changed his wet shoes
and went out again.

47

"Christopher Anthony Jonathan Tuttle,
Don't you step in ONE MORE puddle!"

So Christopher Anthony Jonathan
changed his wet shirt
and changed his wet pants
and changed his wet socks
and changed his wet shoes
and went out again.

"Christopher Anthony Jonathan Tuttle,
Don't you step in ONE MORE puddle!"

BUT...
he didn't have shoes
and he didn't have socks
and he didn't have pants
and he didn't have shirts.

So Christopher Anthony Jonathan Tuttle
couldn't go out in a single puddle.

Spring Rain

The storm came up so very quick
    It couldn't have been quicker.
I should have brought my hat along,
    I should have brought my slicker.

My hair is wet, my feet are wet,
    I couldn't be much wetter.
I fell into a river once
    But this is even better.

Marchette Chute

52

"Want to go fishing, Hen?" asked Frog.
"Not today, Frog," said Hen.
"Can't you see it's raining?"

"Another day then," said Frog.
And he hopped off toward the pond.
"Maybe I'll ask Cat," said Frog.
So he stopped at Cat's house.

"Want to go fishing, Cat?" asked Frog.
"Not today, Frog," said Cat.
"Can't you see it's raining?"

"Another day then," said Frog.
And he hopped off toward the pond.
"Maybe I'll ask Horse," said Frog.
So he stopped at Horse's house.

"Want to go fishing, Horse?" asked Frog.

"Not today, Frog," said Horse.

"Can't you see it's raining?"

"Another day then," said Frog sadly.
"I'll NEVER find a fishing partner."
And he turned to go home.
On his way, he met Duck.

"Where are you going, Frog?" said Duck.
"Can't you see it's a lovely day to go fishing?"

So Frog and Duck went off to fish and had
a perfectly fine time in the rain.

Rhyme

I like to see a thunder storm,
A dunder storm,
A blunder storm,
I like to see it, black and slow,
Come stumbling down the hills.

I like to hear a thunder storm,
A plunder storm,
A wonder storm,
Roar loudly at our little house
And shake the window sills!

Elizabeth Coatsworth

PAUL ROGERS

What Will The Weather Be Like Today?

PICTURES BY KAZUKO

Just at the moment
when night becomes day,
when the stars in the sky
begin fading away,

you can hear all the birds
and the animals say,

"What will the weather be like today?"

Will it be windy?

Will it be warm?

Will there be snow?

Or a frost?

Or a storm?

"Be dry," says the lizard,

"and I won't complain."

The frog in the bog says,
"Perhaps it will rain."

The white cockatoo
likes it steamy and hot.

The mole doesn't know
if it's raining or not.

"Whatever the weather,
I work," says the bee.

"Wet," says the duck,
"is the weather for me."

"Weather? What's that?"

say the fish in the sea.

The world has awakened.
The day has begun,

and somewhere it's cloudy,

and somewhere there's sun,

and somewhere the sun
and the rain meet to play,

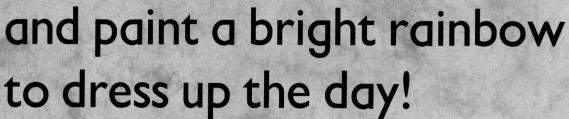

and paint a bright rainbow
to dress up the day!

How is the weather where *you* are today?

Year Round the Raindrops

by Bill Martin Jr
and John Archambault

READ ALOUD

In the early spring,
do the raindrops sing,

READ ALOUD

as they drippy-drop-drip
from the tippy-top-tip
and trickle down the branches
of the pear tree?

On the 4th of July
as the raindrops fly,
are they red-white-and-blue?

Do they Yankee doodle do?

READ ALOUD

Do they boom, do they bang,

and sparkle, too,

like we do?

READ ALOUD

When vacation ends
and school begins,

READ ALOUD

do the raindrops cry
when they say good-bye
to the places they've been
in summer?

READ ALOUD

When winter comes
and numbs the thumbs,
do the raindrops quake?
Do they shiver, do they shake?

READ ALOUD

Do they know they'll soon be snowflakes?

ABOUT THE
Authors & Illustrators

Marchette Chute

Marchette Chute is a poet. She and her sisters grew up in the country. When they were little, they began to write by making books for their dolls. Marchette Chute's poems are favorites of children today.

Taro Gomi

Taro Gomi grew up in Japan. He has drawn pictures for more than 100 children's books. Taro Gomi won a prize for the pictures in the book he wrote, *Spring is Here*.